Families

By Jordan Avery

Glen will tell you about all kinds of families.

Some families are big, and some are small.
One kind of family is not happier than any other kind!

You can have a family of buddies or a pet family!

Families live in big homes and small homes.

Lily lives in this house with her mum and stepdad.

Everyone in a family must help out at home.

Quin has tidied up his stuff to help out.

His room was messier this morning!

This family has twin babies!

The babies are brothers and best buddies.

One baby cries a lot, and one baby is the happiest baby!

Today, both babies are happy.

This big family lives together in the same home.

Pop and Gran fill everyone's bellies with yummy snacks.

Then everyone tries to be silent while Imogen studies!

Chuck is Luna the puppy's dad. He and Luna are a family!

Chuck feels like the luckiest dad.

Luna loves to see other puppies.

But if Luna spies a cat, she tries to catch it!

It can cost a lot to live alone, so sometimes buddies live together. Buddies can be like a family!

Jess's dad sent her a funny text. Jess's buddies laugh as Jess replies to her dad.

This family of two has a new home.

Grant supplied the couch, and Lin brought the rug!

My mum adopted me.
Me, my mum and my two bunnies are a happy family!

CHECKING FOR MEANING

1. How does Quin help at home? *(Literal)*
2. Why do buddies sometimes live together? *(Literal)*
3. Do you think Luna the puppy prefers to see cats or other dogs? *(Inferential)*
4. What would be the best thing about living with some buddies? *(Evaluative)*

EXTENDING VOCABULARY

tidied	Read the word *tidied*. What is the base word of *tidied*? What are some things that you tidy at home or at school?
twin	What does it mean if babies are twins? What would they be called if there were three babies?
spies	What is the base word of *spies*? What is another way of saying *If Luna spies a cat ...*?

MOVING BEYOND THE TEXT

1. This text tells us about many different kinds of families. What other kinds of families do you know?

2. Chuck thinks of Luna the puppy as his family. Do you think pets are part of a family? Why?

3. In many families, each member has a special job to do. What chores do you have at home?

4. Some people like to live alone. What do you think would be some good and bad things about living by yourself? Would you prefer to live alone or with other people?

TIME TO WRITE

Write about a day at your home. Who lives with you? What things happen every day at your home? What is your home like?